Butterflies & Moths

Todd Telander

FALCON GUIDES

GUILFORD, CONNECTICUT
HELENA, MONTANA

AN IMPRINT OF GLOBE PEQUOT PRESS

To my wife, Kirsten; my children, Miles and Oliver; and my parents, all of whom have supported and encouraged me through the years.

To buy books in quantity for corporate use or incentives, call **(800) 962-0973** or e-mail **premiums@GlobePequot.com**.

FALCONGUIDES®

Illustrations by Todd Telander
Text design: Sheryl P. Kober
Project editor: Lauren Brancato
Layout: Mary Ballachino

Library of Congress Cataloging-in-Publication Data is available on file.

ISBN 978-0-7627-7933-8

Printed in the United States of America

10 9 8 7 6 5 4 3 2 1

Butterflies

Moths

Introduction

Butterflies and moths (which together form the group called Lepidoptera, or "scaled wings") are among the most fascinating of insects. Their flight is lovely to watch, their intricate colors and patterns fascinate, and their fragile appearance surprises, given the strength and stamina that allows some species to migrate thousands of miles. Possibly most intriguing is their ability to transform themselves from wormlike caterpillars into delicate, multicolored flying insects.

To aid in the identification process of these unique creatures, it is helpful to first recognize the basic differences between butterflies and moths. Butterflies are generally diurnal (active during the day), are brightly colored, hold their wings closed when at rest, and have thin, club-tipped antennae. Moths are generally nocturnal (active during the night), show pale or dull colors, hold their wings open or folded across the back, and have feathered antennae. The exceptions to these distinctions are too numerous to list, but in most cases these features will guide you to the proper group.

This book is designed to help you identify their magnificent members. Since North America alone is home to upwards of 12,000 species, this book can only serve as an introduction to those you'll be most likely to see—ninety of the more common and interesting Lepidoptera in North America. I hope you enjoy your discovery of these gentle creatures as much as I have enjoyed writing about and painting them.

Notes on the Species Accounts

Names

The common name as well as the scientific name is given at the beginning of each entry. Of the two, the universally accepted scientific name of genus and species is the more reliable identifier, because common names tend to vary regionally, and sometimes there may be more than one, as may be noted in the Description section (see p. vii). For those familiar with Latin, scientific names can also provide valuable clues about the species in question. The Dogbane Tiger Moth's scientific name, *Cycnia tenera*, is a good example. *Cycnia* signifies a kind of swan, and *tenera* means soft or delicate. The translation suggests a moth with soft, swanlike coloring, which in fact is the case.

Families

Butterflies and moths are grouped into families based on similar structures, behaviors, and common ancestry. In the Family section you'll find both the scientific name and the common one for each butterfly or moth's family group. Sometimes a subgroup for the butterfly/moth in question is given too, so you'll know a bit more about exactly where it fits within that larger category. After you are familiar with the more common families and their shared characteristics, you can often place an unfamiliar butterfly or moth into a family, which will reduce your search to a smaller group. For example, if you find a large moth with a large body, short and pointed wings, and a complex wing pattern, you might first look in the family Sphingidae (which includes the sphinx and hawk moths) and narrow your search from there.

Size

Sizes given refer to the wingspan, from forewing tip to forewing tip with the wings outstretched. Of course, when the wings are closed, pulled down, or folded across the back, the wingspan will appear smaller. Use this measurement as a general guide to give a sense of the relative size of your subject, noting that there can be quite a bit of variability between different individuals of the same species, and in many cases, between the male and female.

Habitat
Habitat is the general description of the land, climate, and vegetative features within a butterfly or moth's range. Since many species depend on very specific host plants during the larval stage, their habitat will be strongly linked to where those plants are found. During the adult stage, however, many individuals may disperse or migrate over a wide range of habitats, far away from where the host plant is found. Other species are quite general in their food choices, and can be found almost anywhere within their range.

Range
Range is the geographic area where a species exists. It can be very broad, such as the worldwide area inhabited by the Indian-Meal Moth, or quite limited, like the comparatively much smaller area of California, home to the California Sister. Range is a helpful diagnostic tool, because you can quickly note the species that you are likely to encounter in your area. But also be aware that there are cases when individuals carried by winds, or in migration, are found far from their normal range.

Food
In the Food listings you'll find favored host plants that caterpillars depend upon for survival. Some species use only one kind of plant, while others may feed on multiple plants as well as trees, grains, or wood. As adults, most butterflies feed on nectar from flowering plants that may or may not be related to their host plant. Rotting fruit, moisture and salts from puddles, and even carrion and dung serve as additional sources of nourishment. Many species of moths lack functioning mouthparts as adults, live only for a period of days, and do not feed at all.

Description

The descriptions give plain-language lists of the general features and lifestyles of adults and larvae, though if scientific terms are needed for better accuracy they'll be included. (A diagram of scientifically labeled butterfly/moth parts is provided in the next section.) Within each description you'll find attributes such as wing shape and color of both forewings and hindwings, body shape and color, style of antennae, hairiness, flight behavior, and feeding habits. (Note that mounted specimens may lose much of their color and sometimes their patterning and are often portrayed in very unnatural positions.) For the larvae, the descriptions refer to the mature caterpillar, understanding that younger stages ("instars") of the caterpillar may differ slightly. Attributes include shape, color, presence of protuberances, spines, hairs, and behavior.

Illustrations

The illustrations show the upper side of an average specimen of each species. Use them as a visual guide to overall shape, color, and patterning, bearing in mind that there may be considerable variation in appearance between individuals, particularly between males and females, or for species that have distinct forms in different ranges. Most species are shown with wings outstretched. Although butterflies in nature commonly hold their wings closed, and some moths fold their wings tightly across the back, this presentation communicates the most descriptive information. The underside of the wings is not illustrated, but is described in the text.

Parts of a Butterfly/Moth

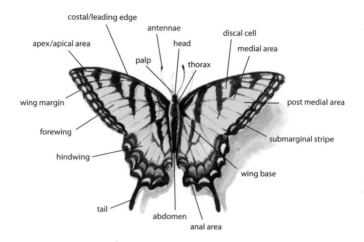

BUTTERFLIES

Pipevine Swallowtail, *Battus philenor*

Family Papilionidae (Swallowtails and Parnassians)

Size: Wingspan 3–5"

Habitat: Woodland edges, streamsides, open fields

Range: Southern latitudes across the contiguous United States and into Mexico

Food: The caterpillar eats the leaves of pipevines and related plants. The adult feeds on flower nectar and nutrients from mud puddles.

Description: The Pipevine Swallowtail is a dark, medium-size, active swallowtail with shallowly scalloped hindwings and moderate tail projections. It is poisonous to predators and thus often mimicked by other butterfly species. The upperside of the forewing is flat black and iridescent, while the upper surface of the hindwing is metallic blue (more developed in males) with pale crescent-shaped spots along its base. The underside hindwing has large, orange, submarginal spots and retains the blue sheen of its upper surface. The body is black with small yellow spots along the sides, and the antennae are thin with clubbed tips. The caterpillar is dark, reddish brown, smooth, and lined with fleshy appendages and orange spots.

Black Swallowtail, *Papilio polyxenes*
Family Papilionidae (Swallowtails and Parnassians)
Size: Wingspan 3–4"
Habitat: Roadsides, sunny fields, meadows
Range: Throughout the contiguous United States
Food: The caterpillar eats the leaves of cow parsnip, Queen Anne's lace, and other plants in the carrot family. Adults feed on nectar from flowers.
Description: The Black Swallowtail is a common dark butterfly with prominent tails and scalloped hindwing margins. The wings are black overall with a prominent, broken, postmedial band of yellow and yellow spotting along the margins. The lower hindwings are iridescent blue (more pronounced in females), each showing an anal spot that is orange with a black center. The wing undersides are marked similarly, but the spotting is more orange than yellow, especially on the hindwings. The body is plump and black, with rows of small yellow spots down the abdomen. The antennae are thin with clubbed tips. The caterpillar is smooth, plump, and green with orange-spotted black bands.

Zebra Swallowtail, *Protographium marcellus*

Family Papilionidae (Swallowtails and Parnassians)

Size: Wingspan 3–4.5"

Habitat: Meadows, streamsides, brushy fields

Range: Throughout eastern and southern United States

Food: The caterpillar eats pawpaw plants (populations are restricted to areas where this plant is present). Adults feed on flower nectar and minerals and salts from mud puddles.

Description: The Zebra Swallowtail is a member of the "kite swallowtails," so called because of their kitelike, triangular shape and their extremely long, pointed tails. The upperside wings are creamy white with continuous black "zebra-stripe" markings. The forewings have smooth margins, while the hindwings have gently scalloped margins, light submarginal spots, light tail tips, and red spots at the inner base. The underside of each hindwing has a distinct red medial stripe. Summer individuals are paler and larger, with longer tails than those seen in spring. The body matches the wings, being striped black and white also. The antennae are thin, club-tipped, and pale. The caterpillar is smooth, pale green with thin dark bands and has an enlarged thoracic region. Zebra Swallowtails generally fly low to the ground.

Giant Swallowtail, *Papilio cresphantes*
Family Papilionidae (Swallowtails and Parnassians)
Size: Wingspan 4–6"
Habitat: Orchards, gardens
Range: Lower latitudes of the eastern United States
Food: The caterpillar eats the leaves of citrus trees (where it is often considered a pest), prickly ash, and hop trees. Adults feed on flower nectar and the salts and moisture from puddles.
Description: The Giant Swallowtail is the largest butterfly in North America, with a very wide wingspan, scalloped hindwings, and long, bulbous tail projections. The upperside wings are dark brown to black overall with a wide yellow band traversing their entire length, and large, yellow submarginal spots across the hindwings and lower forewings. The tails have a distinct yellow spot, and hindwings show orange and blue anal spots. The underside is pale yellow with dark markings along cell borders and blue crescents on the hindwing. The caterpillar is smooth, mottled brown and white, and has orange, forked horns that release a foul scent. Giant Swallowtails fly high with slow flight and long glides.

Eastern Tiger Swallowtail, *Papilio glaucus*

Family Papilionidae (Swallowtails and Parnassians)

Size: Wingspan 3–5.5"

Habitat: Gardens, parks, riversides, forest clearings

Range: Throughout eastern United States

Food: The caterpillar eats the leaves of trees, including those from the rose, magnolia, laurel, and willow families. Adults feed on flower nectar and the salts and moisture from puddles.

Description: Among the largest of North American butterflies, the Eastern Tiger Swallowtail is common throughout its range, is diurnal, and—typical of this family—has distinct projections or "tails" on the hindwings. When alighted and/or feeding, the wings may be seen to tremble. Both sexes are bright yellow above and show ragged black stripes, like those of a tiger, along the anterior forewings, and black marginal patterning on both fore- and hind-wings. The first submarginal spot on the hindwing is orange. The underside is patterned similarly but is much paler yellow. Females show bright blue posterior markings, and in some southern individuals, may be nearly black overall (and look similar to the Spicebush Swallowtail). Like the wings, the body also has black and yellow stripes. The caterpillar is brown to greenish, smooth, and plump. The adult female is illustrated.

Clodius Parnassian, *Parnassius clodius*
Family Papilionidae (Swallowtails and Parnassians)
Size: Wingspan 2–2.5"
Habitat: Open woodlands, mountain meadows, coastal areas
Range: Northwestern United States from central California to the northern Rocky Mountains
Food: The caterpillar eats plants of the bleeding heart family (Fumariaceae), feeding during the night and resting near the ground during the day. Adults feed on flower nectar.
Description: The Clodius Parnassian, a pale butterfly with rounded wings, is related to swallowtails but lacks the familiar tail projections on the hindwings. The wings are creamy white overall, with various gray striations and three distinct dark-gray bands in the discal cell (there are no red spots, as in the similar Phoebus Parnassian). The hindwing has two red spots bordered by black and a dark inner region. Females may exhibit a thin red line at the inner base. The underside is marked similarly. The body is a mixture of creamy white and dark gray, and the antennae are short, black, and club-tipped. The caterpillar is black, covered with short hair, and has rows of small yellow spots near the base. The adult female is illustrated.

Orange Sulfur, *Colias eurytheme*

Family Pieridae (Sulfurs and Whites)
Size: Wingspan 1.5–2.5"
Habitat: Meadows, fields, farmlands, roadsides
Range: Throughout the contiguous United States
Food: The caterpillar eats alfalfa and clover. Adults feed on flower nectar.

Description: Also known as the Alfalfa Butterfly, this common butterfly is often found in dense, low-flying groups over alfalfa fields, where it is often considered a pest. The upperside wings are yellow and extensively washed with bright orange. A wide, dark band occurs along the outer margins of both fore- and hindwings, a reddish discal spot appears on the hindwing, and a distinct, black discal spot sits on the forewing. The dark margin in females is broken by irregular orange markings. The underside is yellow with a red-bordered white discal spot on the hindwing, accompanied by a smaller spot just above it. The body is pale yellow below, darker above, and the club-tipped antennae are reddish. The caterpillar is thin, smooth, and green, with a pale longitudinal stripe down each side. This species is similar to the Clouded, or Common Sulfur, which has a lemon yellow rather than orange cast, and lacks the hindwing spot. The illustration shows the adult male.

Cabbage Butterfly, *Pieris rapae*
Family Pieridae (Sulfurs and Whites)
Size: Wingspan 1.3–1.75"
Habitat: Open fields, farmlands, roadsides
Range: Throughout the contiguous United States
Food: The caterpillar eats cabbage and other plants of the mustard (Brassicaceae) family, including Nasturtium sp. Also known as a "cabbage worm," it is considered a major pest to crops. Adults feed on flower nectar.
Description: Also known as the Cabbage White or Small White, the Cabbage Butterfly is a hardy, nonnative species introduced to North America in the late 1800s and now found across the continent. The upperside wings are plain, creamy white with gray to black apical patches and show a distinct dark spot on the center of the forewings and upper margins of the hindwings. Females have an additional spot on the forewing, below the first. The underside is pale yellow to yellow green. Early broods of this species tend to be paler with fewer dark markings than late broods. The body is dark above, paler below, with long hairs, especially on the thorax. The antennae are thin and club tipped. The caterpillar is pale green with thin, longitudinal yellow stripes and a delicate, bumpy-hairy surface. The illustration depicts the adult female.

9

Pine White, *Neophasia menapia*
Family Pieridae (Sulfurs and Whites)
Size: Wingspan 1.5–2.25"
Habitat: Coniferous forests to subalpine elevations
Range: Western half of the contiguous United States
Food: The caterpillar eats the needles of conifers, especially those of Douglas-fir, balsam fir, Jeffrey pine, and ponderosa pine. Adults feed on flower nectar.
Description: The Pine White is a small, white butterfly with rounded wings, often found flying high in the canopy of pine and fir trees. The upperside wings are creamy white overall with a dark gray costal margin, discal spot, and an outer margin broken by white spots. The hindwings have faint, darker lines along the wing veins; these are more pronounced on their undersides. The female's wings are paler than the male's, and their undersides are yellow-tinged, with thin, pinkish margins on the hindwings. The body is mottled white and gray and has thin, club-tipped antennae. The caterpillar is small and green with white stripes along the top and sides. This butterfly drops from a tree on a silken thread to pupate on the ground. The adult male is illustrated.

Checkered White, *Pontia protodice*

Family Pieridae (Sulfurs and Whites)

Size: Wingspan 1.3–2"

Habitat: A variety of open places, fields, roadsides

Range: Throughout the contiguous United States, most commonly in southern latitudes

Food: The caterpillar eats mustard, cabbage, and other plants of the mustard family (Brassicaceae). Adults feed on flower nectar.

Description: Also known as the Southern Cabbage Butterfly, the Checkered White is a small butterfly with jittery, active flight and pronounced sexual dimorphism. The female is off-white, extensively marked overall in a dull gray to gray-brown checkered pattern. The male is cleaner white, less extensively marked, but with a prominent black discal spot and smaller spot in the apical region of the forewing. The underside is similar to the upperside, but in females the darker markings are a pale, greenish brown that fades into gray. The body is mottled white and dark gray and is lighter below. The thin, club-tipped antennae end in light spots. The caterpillar is greenish with longitudinal yellowish stripes, and is covered in black, warty spots. The illustration shows the adult female.

Falcate Orangetip, *Anthocharis midea*

Family Pieridae (Sulfurs and Whites)

Size: Wingspan 1.5–1.75"

Habitat: Moist woodlands, streamsides, open fields

Range: Eastern and central United States, north to Great Lakes region, and east to Texas

Food: The caterpillar eats cress and other plants of the mustard family (Brassicaceae), choosing buds, flowers, and seedpods rather than leaves. Adults feed on flower nectar.

Description: The Falcate Orangetip is a small, white butterfly with a distinctive hooked (falcated) margin to the outer forewing, and lazy, low-to-the-ground flight. The upperside wings of both sexes are white overall with a black spot in the discal forewing cell and black marks at the apical margins. The male has solid-orange apical regions; this color is absent in females. The undersides of the hindwings are extensively marbled with dark, yellowish green. The body is mottled blackish and light gray, with pale, thin, club-tipped antennae. The caterpillar is green with fine, black, warty spots and two prominent white medial stripes. The illustration depicts the adult male.

Southern Dogface, *Zerene cesonia*

Family Pieridae (Sulfurs and Whites)
Size: Wingspan 2–3″
Habitat: Dry fields, open woodlands, farmlands
Range: Coast to coast of mostly southern continental United States, but reaching as far north as the Great Lakes region
Food: The caterpillar eats clover, false indigo, and other plants of the pea family (Fabaceae). Adults feed on flower nectar.
Description: The Southern Dogface is a striking sulfur butterfly with rapid flight, pointed wingtips, and straight outer margins to the forewings. It is similar to the California Dogface, which is restricted to a small range in western California. The male is yellow overall with broad, black patches at the base and outer margin of its forewings, which also show a black discal spot. These markings together give the crude appearance of the head of a poodle-like dog. The hindwing has a black outer marginal band with two faint, white, orange-bordered spots near the center. The female is a plain, dull yellow with black forewing spots and may show pinkish patterning on her underside hindwing. The body is mottled yellow and black, darker above than below, and has thin, club-tipped antennae. The caterpillar is smooth, green, and variably marked with yellow and black rings and/or whitish, longitudinal stripes down each side, with an overall covering of small, blackish warts. The illustration shows the adult male.

Harvester, *Feniseca tarquinius*

Family Lycaenidae (Gossamer-wings: Blues, Coppers, and Hairstreaks)

Size: Wingspan 1–1.25"

Habitat: Moist, deciduous woodlands, principally near alders

Range: Throughout the eastern half of the contiguous United States

Food: The caterpillar is the only North American carnivorous caterpillar, eating woolly aphids associated with alder, hawthorn, and beech trees. It does not eat leaves. Adults feed on honeydew from aphids and the salts and moisture from damp soil.

Description: The Harvester is a small, relatively uncommon butterfly, and the only member of its subfamily in North America. The wings have pointed tips and convex forewing margins. The sexes are similar, with a rich, orange upperside that has substantial dark brown patches and spots on both forewings and hindwings. The wing undersides are pale brownish orange with many darker circular spots outlined in white. The body, brownish above and white below, is plump and short with black-and-white spotted, thin, club-tipped antennae. The caterpillar is fat, sluglike, and dull green, with obvious segmentations, and covered with fine hairs. It resides below a silky net that includes aphid carcasses.

American Copper, *Lycaena phlaeas*
Family Lycaenidae (Gossamer-wings: Blues, Coppers, and Hairstreaks)
Size: Wingspan 1–1.25"
Habitat: Meadows, roadsides, fields
Range: Throughout the contiguous United States but most commonly in the northern and eastern regions
Food: The caterpillar feeds on various sorrels and docks. Adults feed on flower nectar.
Description: The American Copper is a small, beautiful, common butterfly with a fairly aggressive disposition. The wing patterning is variable, but generally the upperside forewing is coppery-orange with a dark marginal band and several black spots. The hindwing is mostly blackish or dark brown with an orange basal band. A thin, pale margin is present on both sets of wings. The underside wings are similar but much paler overall. The sexes are similar, although some females may show bluish markings above the orange band on the hindwing. The body is dark brown above, pale grayish below, with dark, club-tipped antennae dotted with white. The caterpillar is sluglike, variously colored pale greenish to reddish and covered with fine hairs. The adult female is illustrated.

Purplish Copper, *Lycaena helloides*

Family Lycaenidae (Gossamer-wings: Blues, Coppers, and Hairstreaks)
Size: Wingspan 1–1.5"
Habitat: Variety of habitats including meadows, roadsides, and stream sides
Range: From California to the Midwest in sea-level to alpine areas
Food: The caterpillar feeds on leaves of docks and sorrels, including knotweed and cinquefoil. Adults feed on flower nectar.

Description: The Purplish Copper is a close relative to the American Copper, but with a western range. The upperside wings of the male are coppery orange flushed with iridescent purple, a color combination which can appear brownish to nearly pink. They have scattered black spots, a wide, dark, submarginal band, and orange crescents along the base of the hindwing. There is a thin, whitish margin to both wings. The female is patterned similarly but with an overall orange (not purple) cast, and wider, dark forewing bands. The underside of both sexes is paler and sometimes tinted yellow. The body is stout, dark gray brown above, lighter below, and has thin, black-and-white-dotted, club-tipped antennae. The caterpillar is green, sluglike, and has dark, longitudinal stripes. The adult male is illustrated.

Blue Copper, *Lycaena heteronea*

Family Lycaenidae (Gossamer-wings: Blues, Coppers, and Hairstreaks)
Size: Wingspan 1.1–1.4"
Habitat: Alpine meadows, open brush, sage-covered land
Range: Throughout the western contiguous United States, most commonly at higher elevations
Food: The caterpillar feeds on the leaves of buckwheat. Adults feed on flower nectar, principally that of buckwheat.
Description: The Blue Copper is an unusual member of the copper group because of its blue color. Sometimes confused with one of the "blue" butterflies, it can be distinguished by its noticeably larger size. The upperside wings of the male are a brilliant sky blue with white margins; thin, black submarginal bands; and darkened veins. The female's upper wings are blue gray to brown with several small, dark, interior spots on both wings. The undersides of both sexes are pale grayish to yellowish with dark spotting (usually more pronounced on females). The body is stout, hairy, dark gray above and paler below, with thin, black-and-white-dotted, club-tipped antennae. The caterpillar is pale green and covered with fine, whitish hairs. The illustration represents the adult male.

Gray Hairstreak, *Strymon melinus*

Family Lycaenidae (Gossamer-wings: Blues, Coppers, and Hairstreaks)

Size: Wingspan 1–1.25″

Habitat: Fields, open rural areas, disturbed sites

Range: Throughout the contiguous United States

Food: The caterpillar eats the fruits, flowers, leaves, and seedpods of a variety of plants including legumes, mallow, and cotton, often boring into its food. Adults feed on flower nectar.

Description: The swift-flying Gray Hairstreak is the most common hairstreak in North America. Hairstreaks are so called because of the usual presence of thin streaks along the undersides of the wings. They also usually have one or two thin tails on each hindwing. The upperside wings are overall slate gray (browner in females) with white margins. When there are two tails, they are uneven in length, and accompanied near their base by a large orange spot above a smaller black dot. The underside is pale brown gray with black streaking, bordered with white and orange. The body is stout, grayish above and paler gray below, and has black-and-white-dotted, antennae tipped with orange. The caterpillar is pale green to brownish, plump, and covered with fine whitish hairs. The illustration shows the adult male.

Colorado Hairstreak, *Hypaurotis crysalus*

Family Lycaenidae (Gossamer-wings: Blues, Coppers, and Hairstreaks)
Size: Wingspan 1.25–1.5"
Habitat: Oak woodlands, canyons, scrub
Range: Utah, Colorado, New Mexico, and Arizona, and south into north-central Mexico
Food: The caterpillar eats mostly the leaves of Gambel's oak. Adults feed on the honeydew of aphids, tree sap, and sometimes flower nectar.

Description: The Colorado Hairstreak is one of the larger hairstreaks, and it often rests high in the canopy of oak trees. Like most hairstreaks, it has wispy tails and an adjacent, shorter tail projection on the hindwings. Wing color and patterning are similar in males and females: The upperside wings are bright violet with a broad, dark, blackish-brown band at the margins and thin, white edges. There are orange spots at the outer angle of the forewings and at the base of the hindwings. Undersides are pale brown to gray, with several white "hairstreak" lines and a jagged one on the hindwing that resembles the letter "M." The body is dark gray above, lighter below, with black-and-white-dotted, thin, club-tipped antennae. The caterpillar is plump, light green, and covered with fine, whitish hairs.

19

Coral Hairstreak, *Satyrium and titus*

Family Lycaenidae (Gossamer-wings: Blues, Coppers, and Hairstreaks)
Size: Wingspan 1–1.5"
Habitat: Brushy areas, streamsides, roadsides, thickets
Range: Throughout the contiguous United States except for the southwest region, most commonly in the East
Food: The caterpillar remains on the ground during the day and feeds at night on the leaves and fruit of wild cherry and plum. Adults feed on flower nectar, especially that of butterfly weed, rabbitbrush, and dogbane.
Description: The Coral Hairstreak is one of many similar, small hairstreaks. Males have rather pointed forewings, females have more rounded ones, and both sexes lack tails but have elongated hindwings. The upperside is plain, dark brown overall, although some individuals may show faint orange spotting along the outer wing borders. The underside is light brown to gray brown with a row of coral, circular spots near the outer margin of the hindwing and black, white-bordered spots farther inward on both wings. The body is dark brown gray above, paler below, with thin, black-and-white-dotted, club-tipped antennae. The caterpillar is light green, sluglike, and often accompanied by ants. The illustration shows the adult male.

Great Purple Hairstreak, *Atlides halesus*

Family Lycaenidae (Gossamer-wings: Blues, Coppers, and Hairstreaks)
Size: Wingspan 1.4–2"
Habitat: Hardwood forests (especially oak and walnut) with mistletoe growth
Range: Lower latitudes of the contiguous United States, California to Virginia
Food: The caterpillar eats the leaves of mistletoe. Adults feed on flower nectar.
Description: The Great Purple Hairstreak is one of the most brilliant of North American butterflies. It is a large hairstreak with one long and one shorter tail on each hindwing, and females are generally larger than males. The upperside wings are iridescent blue (not really purple), brightest in males, with broad marginal bands of velvety black. The forewings show a black discal spot, while the hindwings have white marks at their outer angles above the tails. The undersides are dull grayish purple with bright red-orange spots at the bases of both wings. The body is blue above, while the underside of the abdomen is reddish orange. The caterpillar is sluglike, green, and finely hairy, with two pale yellow stripes along the bottom sides and a curious diamond-shaped spot near the head. It closely resembles the leaves of the mistletoe plant. The illustration shows the adult male.

Eastern Tailed Blue, *Cupido comyntas*

Family Lycaenidae (Gossamer-wings: Blues, Coppers, and Hairstreaks)
Size: Wingspan .75–1.1"
Habitat: Open fields, roadsides, meadows, disturbed areas
Range: Throughout most of eastern United States with scattered populations in California, the Southwest, and the Northwest
Food: The caterpillar eats the leaves of plants in the pea family (Fabaceae), including clover, alfalfa, and false indigo. Adults feed on flower nectar and minerals from puddles.

Description: The Eastern Tailed Blue, along with the Western Tailed Blue, is the only butterfly in the group known as "blues" to have tails. The wings of the male are bright violet blue on the upperside, with white-fringed edges and thick, black, submarginal bands. Above the short, wispy tail on the hindwing are a pair of orange, crescent-shaped spots. The upperside of the female varies from dull gray to dark brown overall, with similar orange markings on the hindwings. In both sexes, the underside is pale gray to brownish with many black, white-bordered spots. The body is hairy, dark bluish gray to brown above and paler below, with black-and-white, thin, club-tipped antennae. The caterpillar is green and finely hairy, with pale lateral stripes and a dark stripe down the back. It secretes honeydew and is often accompanied by ants. The illustration shows the adult male.

Little Metalmark, *Calephelis virginiensis*
Family Riodinidae (Metalmarks)
Size: Wingspan 0.6–1"
Habitat: Grassy fields, meadows, open pine woodlands
Range: Southeastern United States, most commonly farther south
Food: The caterpillar rests on the ground in leaf litter during the day and becomes active at night or in low light to feed on plants in the sunflower family (Asteraceae), including yellow thistle and vanilla leaf. Adults feed on flower nectar.

Description: The Little Metalmark is a tiny metalmark of the group called scintillant metalmarks, known for their shiny, metallic scales and habit of resting with their wings outstretched (often while perched with their heads pointing down). In both sexes, the upperside wings are rusty orange overall and heavily patterned with black or dark gray spots and lines. A distinctive double row of silvery, metallic marks follows the wing contours. The underside is patterned as above, but is paler. The body color is similar to that of the wings, and the thin, club-tipped antennae, typically held close together, are dotted black and white. The caterpillar is pale green with black spots along the sides, and covered in fine, long hairs.

Mormon Metalmark, *Apodemia mormo*
Family Riodinidae (Metalmarks)
Size: Wingspan 0.8–1.3"
Habitat: Deserts and other arid, rocky areas
Range: Western region of the contiguous United States except for the far Northwest
Food: The caterpillar eats the leaves and stems of plants in the buckwheat family (Polygonaceae). Adults feed on flower nectar, particularly that of rabbitbrush and others in the sunflower family (Asteraceae).
Description: The striking Mormon Metalmark is a member of the group known as checkered metalmarks, is very active, and will often rest with its wings outstretched. The female is larger than the male with broader wings but otherwise similar. The upperside wings are rusty orange on the inner portion of the forewing, dark brown to blackish elsewhere, with extensive white spotting overall and checkering on the wing margins. The underside is patterned as above but set against a much paler background color. The body is dark brown above and whitish below; the head has thin, club-tipped antennae and unusual green eyes. The caterpillar is plump; patterned in brown, purplish and black; and has long, thin hairs.

Monarch, *Danaus plexippus*
Family Nymphalidae (Brush-footed Butterflies): Milkweed Butterflies group
Size: Wingspan 3–4.5"
Habitat: Sunny, open fields as well as meadows and gardens. During migration, can be found in almost any environment.
Range: Throughout the contiguous United States to north-central Mexico
Food: The caterpillar eats leaves and flowers of milkweed. Adults feed on flower nectar. Both store toxins from milkweed that make them distasteful to predators.
Description: The Monarch is a large, sturdy, long-lived butterfly most well known for one of the most incredible migratory journeys of the animal kingdom—its yearly flight to Mexico in which millions of this species gather in discrete, isolated locations. The uppersides of the wings are deep orange with wide, black stripes along the veins and black margins infused with a double row of white spots. Males have narrower black vein markings than females, as well as a small, dark "sex spot" near the base of each hindwing. The underside is marked as above, but the orange is paler. The body is black with white spots on the head and thorax, with thin, club-tipped antennae. The caterpillar is fat; smooth; ringed with black, white, and yellow bands; and has black tentacles behind the head. The adult male is shown.

Queen, *Danaus gilippus*

Family Nymphalidae (Brush-footed Butterflies): Milkweed Butterflies group
Size: Wingspan 2.75–3.3"
Habitat: Open fields, roadsides, streamsides, desert
Range: Southwestern United States across to Gulf and South Atlantic coastal states
Food: The caterpillar eats leaves of various milkweeds. Adults feed on flower nectar. Both store toxins from milkweed that make them distasteful to predators.
Description: The Queen is similar to the Monarch but is slightly smaller and more subdued in color and pattern and does not migrate. The upper sides of its wings are brownish orange overall with broad, black, marginal bands across the leading, side, and bottom edges. There are several white spots on the outer half of the forewing and within the margin, and males show a dark spot of sex scales near the base of the hindwing. Some southwest individuals have whitish venation on the hindwing. The wing undersides are patterned similarly but show thicker, blackish vein markings, especially on the hindwing. The body is black with white spots on the head and thorax, and reddish brown on the abdomen. The caterpillar is plump; smooth; off-white with thin, transverse bands of black and yellow; and three pairs of long, fleshy tentacles. The illustration shows the adult male.

Viceroy, *Limenitis archippus*

Family Nymphalidae (Brush-footed Butterflies): Admirals and Sisters group
Size: Wingspan 2.5–3"
Habitat: Meadows, roadsides
Range: Throughout the contiguous United States, most commonly in eastern and southwestern states
Food: The caterpillar eats the leaves and catkins of a variety of trees including cottonwood, willow, poplar, aspen, and wild plum. Adults feed on aphid honeydew, flower nectar, carrion, and dung.

Description: Well known for its uncanny resemblance to the Monarch and Queen, the Viceroy presumably mimics these species because they are distasteful and avoided by predators. The upperside wings are deep orange overall with wide, black venation and margins. White spots dot the dark, marginal bands, and there is an oblique line of black across the middle of the hindwing, which is absent in the Monarch and Queen. The underside is patterned similarly but is duller orange, especially on the hindwings. Sexes are similar. The body is black above, while below it is spotted and striped with white. The caterpillar is rather grotesque: It is mottled creamy white, pale green, and brown; lumpy; and has branched tentacles on the head. These characteristics together give it the appearance of a bird dropping. Viceroys glide with wings held flat, whereas Monarchs keep their wings at an angle.

Red-spotted Purple, *Limenitis arthemis*

Family Nymphalidae (Brush-footed Butterflies): Admirals and Sisters group
Size: Wingspan 2.5–3.75"
Habitat: Deciduous woodlands
Range: Throughout eastern United States
Food: The caterpillar eats the leaves of a variety of trees including wild cherry, willow, poplar, oak, and hawthorn. Adults feed on rotting fruit, dung, and moist soils.

Description: The Red-spotted Purple is the same species as the White Admiral, which has a very different color pattern and ranges farther north, although the two may hybridize to create intermediate forms where their ranges overlap. The Red-spotted Purple superficially resembles the Pipevine Swallowtail, but lacks the tails. The upperside wings are dark blue to black, fading to iridescent blue or blue green near the margins and most of the hindwing. There are reddish spots along the apex of the forewing. The underside is bluish to brown, with several, black-bordered orange spots. The body is a dark blue gray marked with white underneath. The caterpillar, like that of the Viceroy, is often said to resemble a bird dropping: It is cream colored, mottled with dull brown or gray, lumpy, and has two thick tentacles.

California Sister, *Adelpha californica*

Family Nymphalidae (Brush-footed Butterflies): Admirals and Sisters group
Size: Wingspan 2.5–3.5"
Habitat: Oak woodlands and adjacent streamsides
Range: Pacific States (especially California) of the contiguous United States
Food: The caterpillar eats the leaves of various oaks, ingesting compounds that make it distasteful to predators. Adults feed on rotting fruit, tree sap, flower nectar (rarely) and moisture and salts from soil.

Description: The California Sister is a striking, medium-to-large butterfly with relatively long, narrow forewings. It was previously considered the same species as the Arizona Sister (found in Arizona) and the Bredow's Sister (found in Mexico). The upperside wings are velvety black or dark brown with a broad, white, medial band across both wings and a large orange patch at the forewing apex. Sometimes there are deep blue and reddish marks near the base of the leading edge. The underside has a similar pattern; in addition, strips of pale violet blue can be seen near the outer margins and near the bases of both wings. The body is black above, paler below, and has dark, oblique stripes. The caterpillar is thick and pale green, with long tubercules known as "horns."

Red Admiral, *Vanessa atalanta*

Family Nymphalidae (Brush-footed Butterflies): Ladies group
Size: Wingspan 1.75–2.5"
Habitat: A wide variety of open habitats, especially moist areas
Range: Throughout the contiguous United States
Food: The caterpillar eats the leaves of plants in the nettle family (Urticaceae). Adults feed on flower nectar (especially thistles), tree sap, moisture from soil, and rotting fruit.

Description: The Red Admiral is not technically an admiral, but a member of the "ladies" or "thistle butterflies" group. The upperside wings are a deep velvety brownish black with orange (not red) medial bands and white apical spots on the forewings, and broad, orange, marginal bands on the hindwings. Individuals of spring broods are lighter overall, while those of fall broods are darkest. The underside of the forewing is similar to its upper side, while the underside of the hindwing is cryptically mottled with grays. The body is black overall, with club-tipped antennae, ending with light dots. The caterpillar varies from pale green to blackish, is covered with tiny white spots, and has many branched spines. The illustration shows the adult's darker "fall" form.

Painted Lady, *Vanessa cardui*

Family Nymphalidae (Brush-footed Butterflies): Ladies group
Size: Wingspan 2–2.5"
Habitat: Open habitats, gardens, fields, alpine meadows
Range: Throughout the contiguous United States
Food: The caterpillar eats a wide variety of plants including thistles, nettles, burdock, hollyhock, and mallow, enabling it to thrive in most areas. Adults feed on flower nectar.

Description: The Painted Lady is a medium-size, wide-ranging, common butterfly that can be found around the world, so it is sometimes called the "Cosmopolitan." It has strong but erratic flight and is capable of long migrations. The upperside wings are pale orange brown with extensive black markings. A black apical region on the forewing contains several white spots, and small blue spots may be visible at the inner base of the hindwing. The underside forewing is patterned as above, but the hindwing is mottled in earth tones with a row of submarginal eyespots. The body is speckled light and dark brown above, is whitish below, and has thin, club-tipped antennae ending in pale dots. The caterpillar is blackish with pale yellow stripes, and is covered in fine hairs and bristles.

Buckeye, *Junonia coenia*

Family Nymphalidae (Brush-footed Butterflies): True Brushfoot group
Size: Wingspan 1.75–2.5"
Habitat: Open fields, meadows, coastal shores
Range: Throughout the contiguous United States, most commonly in southern latitudes
Food: The caterpillar eats the leaves, buds, and fruit of plaintains, gerardias, and snapdragons. Adults feed on flower nectar, and moisture from mud and sand.

Description: The Buckeye is a medium-size, common butterfly with pronounced eyespots, which are thought to confuse and deter predators. It tends to remain on or near the ground or low parts of vegetation. The upperside wings are variable shades of brown, with each wing showing one large and one small, multicolored spot. There is also a creamy bar near the apex of the forewing, two orange marks in the discal cell, and scalloped patterning along the entire wing edge. The underside is paler, sometimes achieving a rose cast, with eyespots still visible. The body is tan to dark brown with pale, club-tipped antennae. The caterpillar is mottled black, white, and brown, with dark stripes above, and is covered in black, branched spines.

Question Mark, *Polygonia interrogationis*

Family Nymphalidae (Brush-footed Butterflies): True Brushfoot group

Size: Wingspan 2.3–3"

Habitat: Deciduous forests, parks, gardens

Range: Most of the United States east of the Continental Divide

Food: The caterpillar eats the leaves of plants including nettles, elm, hackberry, and hops. Adults feed on tree sap, rotted fruit, flower nectar (rarely) and moisture and salts from soil.

Description: The Question Mark is the largest of the group known as "anglewings," so-called for their ragged, angled, wing margins. The coloration varies depending on the season. Upperside wings on spring forms are bright orange, fading to deep reddish brown near the margins, with several black spots on the inner wing. The wing edges are pale violet, and the hindwing has a prominent, violet-tipped tail. Unlike the bright upper surfaces, the wing undersides show the mottled grays and browns of dead leaves. On the hindwing these drab colors are interrupted by a tiny, silvery arc and dot in the discal area that looks like a question mark—hence its common name. The autumn forms (which overwinter in tree cavities) are generally darker, especially on the hindwing, and may lack the violet wing margins. In both forms, the body is pale brown overall, with thin, club-tipped antennae. The caterpillar is mottled black and white and is covered with reddish-orange, branched spines. The adult spring form is illustrated.

33

Milbert's Tortoiseshell, *Aglais milberti*

Family Nymphalidae (Brush-footed Butterflies): True Brushfoot group
Size: Wingspan 1.75–2.5"
Habitat: Moist meadows, fields, streamsides, open woodlands
Range: Across western continental United States (including Alaska) and northern latitudes of eastern United States into Canada
Food: The caterpillar eats the leaves of plants in the nettle family (Urticaceae). Adults feed on rotting fruit, tree sap, flower nectar (rarely) and moisture and salts from soil.

Description: The Milbert's Tortoiseshell is a medium-size butterfly with angular, ragged wing margins and squared-off wingtips. It is also known as the Fire-rim Tortoiseshell because of its flame-colored patterning. The upperside wings are deep brown with a broad, yellow-orange submarginal band and a dark margin across both wings. On the hindwing there are pale blue spots nestled in the dark outer margin, and the forewing has a white spot at its tip. The underside is patterned similarly but in finely variegated earth tones that produce a dead-leaf appearance. The body is dark brown overall with club-tipped antennae that end in white dots. The caterpillar is pale green with blackish longitudinal bands punctuated with branched spines. It feeds communally in a web when young.

Mourning Cloak, *Nymphalis antiopa*

Family Nymphalidae (Brush-footed Butterflies): True Brushfoot group
Size: Wingspan 2.25–3.5"
Habitat: Deciduous woodlands, parks, rural gardens
Range: Throughout temperate North America
Food: The caterpillar eats the leaves of a variety of broadleaf trees, including willow, poplar, elm, birch, and hackberry. Adults feed on rotting fruit, tree sap, flower nectar (rarely), and moisture and salts from soil.

Description: The Mourning Cloak is a common butterfly with the angular, jagged wing margins typical of the tortoiseshells. The adult overwinters in tree cavities, emerging the following spring to breed. The upperside wings are deep burgundy brown with wide, pale yellow margins. Inside the margin are light blue spots surrounded by black. The underside is dark gray with the same yellowish margin, though on this side it is speckled with black. The body is stout and dark brown to blackish both above and below, with thin, club-tipped antennae. The caterpillar is black, covered with spines, and has small white dots and a row of reddish spots along the back.

Pearl Crescent, *Phyciodes tharos*

Family Nymphalidae (Brush-footed Butterflies): True Brushfoot group

Size: Wingspan 1–1.5"

Habitat: Meadows, fields, gardens, roadsides

Range: Throughout most of the contiguous United States but rare in the Pacific Northwest

Food: The caterpillar eats the leaves of asters (Asteraceae family). Adults feed on flower nectar from a variety of plants.

Description: The Pearl Crescent is a common and widespread butterfly reminiscent of a small fritillary. There is some seasonal variation in the level of darkness in coloration, but in general its wings' uppersides are deep orange with a broad brownish black marginal band, a complex web of dark patterning in the inner wing, and dark spotting on the outer submarginal area of the hindwing. The underside is mottled light brown to grayish, and the hindwing shows a pale, pearly, crescent-shaped spot, hence the common name. The body is brown to blackish above and paler beneath, with thin, club-tipped antennae. The caterpillar is black with pale stripes down the back and sides and has several rows of brownish spines.

Malachite, *Siproeta stelenes*

Family Nymphalidae (Brush-footed Butterflies): True Brushfoot group
Size: Wingspan 2.5–3.5"
Habitat: Open woodlands, citrus and avocado orchards, gardens, streamsides
Range: Tropical Americas reaching north to southern sections of Texas and Florida
Food: The caterpillar eats plants of the Acanthaceae family, including ruellia and blechum. Adults feed on flower nectar, rotting fruit, tree sap, and carrion.
Description: Named for the rare, green mineral, the Malachite is a beautiful, large butterfly of South and Central America with scalloped wing margins and a short, broad tail on the hindwing. The uppersides of the wings are black with translucent, pale-green marks in a broad band along their interior and spotting along the inner margins. On the underside, the green patterning is similar, but the black is replaced by reddish orange and white. The body is black above and white with oblique dark stripes below, with thin, club-tipped antennae. The caterpillar is black with rows of orange-based, branched spines and two long "antlers" at the head.

Great Spangled Fritillary, *Speyeria cybele*

Family Nymphalidae (Brush-footed Butterflies): Fritillary group

Size: Wingspan 2.5–3.75"

Habitat: Wetlands, fields, streamsides, open woodlands

Range: Throughout the contiguous United States but less common in the lower latitudes and the Southeast

Food: The caterpillar feeds at night, eating the leaves of violets. Adults feed on nectar from coneflowers and the flowers of milkweed and thistles.

Description: The Great Spangled Fritillary is a large, common member of the group known as fritillaries or "silverspots." The upperside wings are brownish orange with variable degrees of darker brown suffusion on the inner half of both wings (this is typically darker in females). There is also a complex pattern of stripes, spots, and crescents along the outer half of the wings. The underside is tannish overall, with several silvery spots (the spangles) on the hindwings. The body is light to dark brown above and pale below, with thin, club-tipped antennae. The caterpillar is black and lined with rows of orange-based branching spines. The illustration shows the adult female.

American Snout, *Libytheana carinenta*
Family Nymphalidae (Brush-footed Butterflies): Snout group
Size: Wingspan 1.5–2"
Habitat: Woodland edges and clearings, fields, roadsides, gardens
Range: Southwestern United States to the east coast, north to the Great Lakes
Food: The caterpillar eats the leaves of the hackberry tree. Adults feed on flower nectar.
Description: The unique American Snout, also called the Southern Snout, has enlarged labial palps that together appear as a long snout. By closing its wings, drawing its antennae close together and angling them toward a branch, this butterfly looks exactly like a dry leaf with a long leafstalk. The forewing margins are squared off and jagged. The uppersides of the wings are dark brown to blackish with broad orange patches along the middle sections. The forewings have prominent white spots in the apical region. The undersides of the hindwings and tips of the forewings are a cryptic, mottled gray, so when the wings are folded they resemble a dead leaf. The body is dark gray brown above, paler below, and the stout antennae are broad tipped. The caterpillar's body is green with yellow stripes, its head is small, and the thorax is enlarged, giving it a hunchbacked appearance.

Gulf Fritillary, *Agraulis vanillae*
Family Nymphalidae (Brush-footed Butterflies): Heliconians group
Size: Wingspan 2.5–3"
Habitat: Open fields, forest clearings, gardens
Range: Throughout the lower half of the contiguous United States, especially the Gulf states.
Food: The caterpillar eats the leaves of passion vines and passion flowers. Adults feed on flower nectar.
Description: The Gulf Fritillary is a medium-to-large butterfly with relatively long, narrow forewings that have concave margins. It is more closely related to the longwings or heleconians than to the true fritillaries. The uppersides of its wings are deep orange with numerous black or dark brown spots and marks; in the central disk of the forewing these encase small white spots. The underside is pale brown, orange at the base of the forewing, and both wings are covered with elongated, silvery-white spots, giving this butterfly the alternate name of Silver-spotted Flambeau. The female is typically darker with more extensive dark spots. The body is brownish orange above and whitish with dark oblique stripes below and has thin, black-and-white banded, club-tipped antennae. The caterpillar is striped brown and orange and has several rows of long, black, branching spines.

Zebra Longwing, *Heliconius charithonia*

Family Nymphalidae (Brush-footed Butterflies): Heliconians group

Size: Wingspan 2.75–3.5"

Habitat: Moist, open woodlands and disturbed areas

Range: Gulf states and coastal southeast to South Carolina

Food: The caterpillar eats the leaves of passion vines. Adults feed on flower nectar and pollen.

Description: The Zebra Longwing, also known as the Zebra Heliconian, or simply Zebra, is an unmistakable member of the subtropical group called heliconians, with a wing shape that is much wider than tall. It is a slow-flying, long-lived butterfly (up to three months) that can be found roosting communally at night. The upperside wings are boldly patterned with yellow "zebra" stripes, set against a jet-black background and also show a row of yellow spots along the lower edge of the hindwing. The underside is similar but with paler yellow stripes, and red spots at the base of the hindwing. The body has a thin abdomen, which is striped black and pale yellow along its length, and the head has large eyes, and thin, club-tipped antennae. The caterpillar is white with small black spots and long, black, hairlike projections.

Variable Checkerspot, *Euphydryas chalcedona*

Family Nymphalidae (Brush-footed Butterflies): Checkerspots group

Size: Wingspan 1.25–2.25"

Habitat: A wide range of habitats including deserts, coastal areas, and mountains

Range: Throughout western contiguous United States, including the Rocky Mountains

Food: The caterpillar eats a variety of plants, including snapdragons, Indian paintbrush, penstemon, and monkey flower. Adults feed on flower nectar.

Description: The Variable Checkerspot, also known as the Chalcedon Checkerspot, is a medium-size butterfly with relatively narrow, pointed forewings and variable coloration depending on location. The upper surfaces of its wings are black to tawny brown and heavily checkered with white spots overall. Red to orange spots dot the wing margins and sometimes are seen in the forewing discal cell. The base of the leading edge of the fore-wing is also reddish. The wing undersides are also heavily spotted, but the background color is brownish orange. The body is black above with red-orange marks on its underside, white spots on the abdomen, and more orange-red marks on the palps. Yellow, bulbous clubs sit at the tips of the antennae. The caterpillar is black with white spots or stripes and is lined with fine, bristly spines that arise from orange bases.

Common Wood-Nymph, *Cercyonis pegala*

Family Nymphalidae (Brush-footed Butterflies): Satyrs and Wood-Nymphs group

Size: Wingspan 2–3"

Habitat: Grassy fields, open woodlands, meadows

Range: Throughout most of the contiguous United States except parts of the Northwest, Southwest, and southern Florida

Food: The caterpillar eats a variety of grasses, including oatgrass and bluegrass. Adults feed on flower nectar and rotting fruit.

Description: The Common Wood-Nymph, also known as the Grayling, is a relatively large member of the group that includes satyrs. It has broad, rounded forewings and hindwings with scalloped margins. The upperside wings are colored pale brown to nearly black and carry distinctive black eyespots: two large ones on the forewing and a smaller one on the hindwing. Individuals in the southeast have forewing spots that are surrounded by a broad, pale-yellow apical patch, which is darker or missing altogether in western and northern individuals. The underside is similar on the forewing but variegated gray and brown on the hindwing, often with several eyespots. The body is brown to dark brown above, paler below, and has short antennae with thin, clubbed tips. The caterpillar is finely haired and green with longitudinal yellow stripes. The body tapers at both ends and has a red, forked-tail protuberance. The adult southeastern form is illustrated.

43

Little Wood-Satyr, *Megisto cymela*

Family Nymphalidae (Brush-footed Butterflies): Satyr and Wood-Nymphs group

Size: Wingspan 1.5–2"

Habitat: Open deciduous woodlands and clearings, brushy meadows

Range: Eastern United States

Food: The caterpillar eats a variety of grasses, including orchard grass and bluegrass. Adults feed on flower nectar, tree sap, and aphid secretions.

Description: The Little Wood-Satyr is a small butterfly at home in grassy areas, where it bounds away from intruders and hides under leaves on the ground. The upper surfaces of the wings are pale gray or brown overall, with two prominent, yellow-rimmed black eyespots near the margin of each wing, and multiple, fine, dark lines along the outer margins. The underside is patterned similarly but is paler and carries two brown, central streaks. The body is brown to gray and is paler below, with antennae that have very thin, clubbed tips. The caterpillar is light greenish brown with a dark dorsal stripe, is covered in fine hairs, tapers at both ends, and bears a forked tail projection.

Common Alpine, *Erebia epipsodea*
Family Nymphalidae (Brush-footed Butterflies): Satyr and Wood-Nymphs group
Size: Wingspan 1.6–2"
Habitat: Fields, alpine meadows, open woodlands, marshes
Range: Alaska to northwestern regions of the contiguous United States, into the Rocky Mountains south to New Mexico
Food: The caterpillar eats a variety of grasses and sedges. Adults feed on flower nectar and moisture and salts from wet, sandy soils.
Description: The Common Alpine is a small- to medium-size satyr butterfly with rounded wings, slow, bounding flight, and a preferred habitat in far northern and high altitudes, as its name suggests. The wing uppersides are dark brown overall, and both fore- and hindwing outer regions show black eyespots, often with white centers, surrounded by broad orange patches. The underside has similar eyespots set against a paler brown or mottled gray-and-black background. The body is black above and below, with contrasting white legs and antennae. The caterpillar is light green with a dark dorsal stripe, pale stripes along the sides, a forked tail segment, and a constricted neck region.

Goatweed Leafwing, *Anaea andria*

Family Nymphalidae (Brush-footed Butterflies): Leafwings group
Size: Wingspan 2–3"
Habitat: A variety of open habitats as well as deciduous woodlands
Range: Central and southern United States west to Arizona
Food: The caterpillar eats primarily the leaves of goatweeds. Adults feed on rotting fruit, tree sap, and animal droppings.
Description: True to its name, the Goatweed Leafwing bears a remarkable resemblance to a dried leaf when it is alighted and its wings are folded so that the undersides are revealed. The wingtips are hooked, the outer margins of the forewing are concave, and there is a prominent tail at the base of the hindwing. The uppersides of the wings are bright, rusty orange overall, becoming dark brown near the margins, then white at the edges. The underside is variously plain or mottled in earth tones and resembles a dead leaf. Winter forms are typically darker than summer forms, and wing shape can also vary depending on the season. Females may show a wide, ragged, pale-yellow submarginal band along both fore- and hindwings. The body is brown above and pale below, with thin, club-tipped antennae. The caterpillar is pale green to grayish with numerous tiny, raised bumps. It often rests and feeds in a curled-up leaf.

Tawny Emperor, *Asterocampa clyton*
Family Nymphalidae (Brush-footed Butterflies): Emperors group
Size: Wingspan 1.75–2.75"
Habitat: Areas where hackberries are present, woodland edges, streamsides, gardens
Range: Eastern United States, west to Arizona and north to the Great Lakes region
Food: The caterpillar eats leaves of the hackberry tree. Adults feed on rotting fruit, tree sap, animal droppings, carrion, and salts and moisture from damp soil.
Description: The Tawny Emperor is a medium-size butterfly in a group known as emperors or hackberry butterflies. It is cloaked in a tapestry of warm, soft, earth tones, with the upperside wings having a background color of tawny brown, extensively marked with black, white, and an array of browns. In the male, the hindwing has a row of round, submarginal black spots, an overall dark complexion near the apex, and a concave outer margin to the forewing. In the female, the submarginal spots are absent, the overall complexion is paler, and the outer forewing margin is convex. The underside is patterned similarly but is paler and grayer in both sexes. The body is mottled brown and tawny above, whitish below, and has club-tipped antennae that end in a yellow spot. The caterpillar is pale green with yellowish longitudinal stripes and small pale dots, is covered in fine hairs, and has a forked rear segment; its head has branching antlers.

Long-tailed Skipper, *Urbanus proteus*

Family Hesperiidae (Skippers)
Size: Wingspan 1.75–2.25"
Habitat: Most open habitats, gardens, fields
Range: Gulf and South Atlantic states, most commonly in Florida
Food: The caterpillar eats a variety of plants in the pea family (Fabaceae). Adults feed on flower nectar.

Description: The Long-tailed Skipper is a colorful member of the group known as skippers, so called because their rapid, darting flight resembles skipping. It has a thick, robust body and relatively short wings except for the long, broad tails at the bottom of the hindwings. The upperside wings are dark brown to black, with scattered white spots on the forewing and the margins of both wings. Both wings also have iridescent blue-green scales at their bases. The underside is brownish overall with the same white spots on the forewing. The body is iridescent blue and green with mottled drab earth tones below. The eyes are large, and the antennae are set far apart on the head and end with a hooked tip. The caterpillar is green with tiny yellow spots and a pair of longitudinal yellow stripes, a small, dark-brown head, and a constricted neck region. It is sometimes called the "bean leaf roller" because of its habit of hiding in and feeding on leaves it has rolled up. It can be a pest to bean crops.

Silver-spotted Skipper, *Epargyreus clarus*

Family Hesperiidae (Skippers)
Size: Wingspan 1.75–2.4"
Habitat: Fields, brushy areas, gardens, roadsides
Range: Throughout most of the contiguous United States, especially central and southeastern regions
Food: The caterpillar eats a variety of plants in the pea family (Fabaceae), including locust, wisteria, acacia, and indigo. Adults feed on flower nectar and moisture and salts from sandy soil.
Description: The Silver-spotted Skipper is a medium-to-large skipper with strong flight and blunt, broad, tail projections on the hindwing. The upperside is rich brown overall, with unmarked hindwings and a broken, orange band across the midsection of the forewing. The common name derives from the large, silvery-white patch on the underside of the hindwing. The body is dark brown above and below, robust, with long, fine hairs across the upper thorax, and hooked tips to the antennae. The caterpillar is greenish yellow, mostly smooth, with faint dark bands and a dark reddish-brown head with two red-orange eyespots, and a constricted neck region.

Common Checkered-Skipper, *Pyrgus communis*

Family Hesperiidae (Skippers)

Size: Wingspan 1–1.4"

Habitat: Most open areas, woodland edges, meadows, roadsides

Range: Most of the contiguous United States except the far northwestern region, southern California, and southern Florida

Food: The caterpillar eats a variety of mallows and hollyhocks. Adults feed on flower nectar.

Description: The Common Checkered-Skipper is a widespread skipper with quick, darting flight and an aggressive attitude. As with other skippers, it has a robust body, large eyes, and relatively short wings. The upperside wings are overall light slate gray (in males), blackish (in females), or sometime brownish, and extensively checkered with white spots. The wing margins are also checkered with white. The underside is paler and with similar checkering. The body is brown to gray above, mottled pale gray and white below, with somewhat curving antennae tips. The caterpillar is green to brownish with thin, dark, longitudinal stripes, and is covered with fine, short hairs. It has a dark brown head and a constricted neck area.

Yucca Giant-Skipper, *Megathymus yuccae*
Family Hesperiidae (Skippers)
Size: Wingspan 1.75–3"
Habitat: Desert and semiarid scrub, grasslands, open woodlands
Range: Across lower latitudes of the contiguous United States, north to Utah and Nebraska
Food: The caterpillar eats plants of the yucca family, including Spanish bayonet and Joshua tree, gaining access by boring holes into stalks near the plant base and constructing an upright "tent" at the entrance site. Adults do not feed but may drink water from damp soil and puddles.
Description: The Yucca Giant-Skipper is a member of the giant-skippers group, known for rapid, strong flight and a penchant for dry, desert conditions. The upperside wings are dark brown to charcoal overall, with pale yellow spots on the outer portion of the forewing and a pale-yellow marginal band on the hindwing. Females have additional yellowish spots along the interior of the hindwing and more pointed forewings. The underside is finely mottled in light and dark grays with white spotting. The body is very thick and robust, heavily haired, and colored various shades of gray to brown with a white chin region. The antennae end in thick clubs. The caterpillar is whitish to pale gray brown overall; has a darker, small head; and has a constricted neck region.

MOTHS

Rosy Maple Moth, *Dryocampa rubicunda*
Family Saturniidae (Giant Silk Moths)
Size: Wingspan 1.25–2"
Habitat: Deciduous woodlands
Range: Throughout eastern United States
Food: The caterpillar eats leaves from a variety of broadleaf trees, including maple, oak, and beech. Adults do not feed.
Description: The Rosy Maple Moth is a medium-size moth with a stocky, thick body. The upperside wings are simply patterned pink at the bases and margins, and are pale to bright yellow in between. The underside is patterned similarly but is paler overall. This moth usually holds its wings flat or arched up across the back like a tent. The hairy body is yellow above with pink patches below, is especially thick at the thorax, and has pink legs and broad, orange, feathered antennae. The light green caterpillar has tiny black dots, an orange-red head, and two black tubercules on the front end.

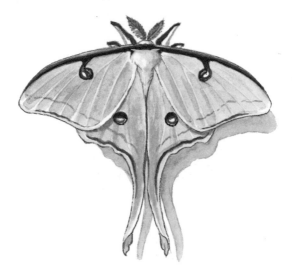

Luna Moth, *Actius luna*

Family Saturniidae (Giant Silk Moths)
Size: Wingspan 3–4.25"
Habitat: Deciduous woodlands
Range: Throughout eastern United States
Food: The caterpillar eats leaves from a variety of broadleaf trees, including oak, walnut, sweetgum, alder, and birch. Adults do not feed.

Description: The Luna Moth is a striking, very large moth with a long, curved tail on each hindwing. The upperside wings are pale yellowish or bluish green with a thin brown stripe across the entire leading edge, and one distinct eyespot on each wing (the forewing spots are continuous with the stripe of the leading edge). The spots resemble moons, giving the moth its common name, Luna. In regions where there are two broods in a year, those of the spring brood have thin, reddish outer margins, while those of the fall brood will have yellow margins. The body is short and fat, is covered in whitish hairs, and has a dark band across the head, dark legs, and feathered antennae. The sexes are similar, but males have wider feathering on the antennae. The caterpillar is plump, light green, and has a yellow stripe across the sides and several rows of dark spots bearing very fine hairs.

Polyphemus Moth, *Antheraea polyphemus*
Family Saturniidae (Giant Silk Moths)
Size: Wingspan 3.5–5.75"
Habitat: Deciduous woodlands, gardens
Range: Throughout the contiguous United States
Food: The caterpillar eats leaves from a variety of broadleaf trees, including oak, willow, apple, hawthorn, and birch. Adults do not feed.

Description: The Polyphemus Moth, a very large, common silk-moth with a stout, heavily furred body, is named for the mythical Cyclops, Polyphemus, who had a single eye. The upperside wings are light to dark brown overall. The forewing has a small, black-bordered, white discal eyespot, small black apical patches, a dark submarginal line, and reddish basal stripe. The hindwing has very large black eyespots encircling yellow, and a broad, dark submarginal stripe. The underside is paler overall with only a suggestion of eyespots. The body is brownish overall, above and below, with feathered antennae, which are more pronounced in the male. The caterpillar is bright green with a brown head, banded with thin yellow stripes, and dotted with orange tubercules bearing thin, dark spines. The illustration shows the adult male.

MOTHS

Cecropia Moth, *Hyalophora cecropia*
Family Saturniidae (Giant Silk Moths)
Size: Wingspan 4–6"
Habitat: Open woodlands, gardens, orchards
Range: Throughout eastern United States and southeastern California
Food: The caterpillar eats leaves from a variety of broadleaf trees, including maple, birch, walnut, plum, and cherry. Adults do not feed.
Description: The Cecropia Moth is a huge silk moth, indeed the largest moth in North America, and is colored with a rich tapestry of reds, browns, and white. The upperside wings have a background color of charcoal brown and pale margins, with both wings showing red-and-white, crescent-shaped spots toward their interiors. The forewing has a black eyespot at the apex. The underside is patterned similarly but is paler overall. The upper surface of the body is reddish brown on the thorax and striped white, red, and black on the abdomen; its underside is spotted below. The legs are orange red, and there is a white collar behind the head. Females have a plump abdomen and thin antennae, while males have narrower abdomens and very bushy antennae. The caterpillar is plump, light green, and has orange tubercles on the head and back and rows of blue tubercles along the sides.

Regal Moth, *Citheronia regalis*
Family Saturniidae (Giant Silk Moths)
Size: Wingspan 3.5–6"
Habitat: Deciduous woodlands, gardens, parks
Range: Throughout eastern United States, especially in the southeastern region
Food: The caterpillar eats leaves from a variety of trees from the walnut family (Juglandaceae), including hickory, walnut, sweet gum, and pecan. Adults do not feed.
Description: The Regal Moth, also known as the Royal Walnut Moth, is a massive, large-bodied moth. The upperside wings have a gray-to-brown background color with scattered, pale-yellow spots on the inner portion; the margins are unmarked. The hindwing is paler and more orange, while the forewing has unusual, red-orange veins. Females are larger than males. The body is well furred, thick, striped reddish and pale yellow on the thorax and banded on the abdomen. The legs are red orange, and the antennae are relatively small and feathery. The caterpillar, known as the hickory horned devil, is very large and imposing, green, marked with black spots and lines, and has several long, arching, red-orange horns on the head and thorax.

MOTHS

Promethea Silkmoth, *Callosamia promethea*
Family Saturniidae (Giant Silk Moths)
Size: Wingspan 2.5–4"
Habitat: Deciduous woodlands, orchards
Range: Throughout eastern United States
Food: The caterpillar eats leaves from a variety of plants, including poplar, tulip tree, sassafras, spicebush, lilac, and white ash. Adults do not feed.

Description: The Promethea Silkmoth is a large silkmoth with notable differences between males and females. The upperside wings of the female are reddish brown with a white line dividing the inner and outer sections and pale brown margins. The forewing has a black apical eyespot, with a small "M-shaped" white line just above it. The inner portions of both wings have a single white chevron. Males are generally much more blackish overall (except on the margins) with thinner forewings that are concave at the outer edge. The body is reddish brown (in females) or blackish (in males) above, paler below, with a white stripe dotted with dark spots along each side. The caterpillar is pale green and plump, with rows of small black spots, thick protuberances on the head, and a single protuberance near the hind end.

Sheep Moth, *Hemileuca eleganterina*
Family Saturniidae (Giant Silk Moths)
Size: Wingspan 2–3"
Habitat: A variety of habitats, including coastal areas, mountains, woodlands, pastures, and scrubland
Range: West of the Continental Divide in the contiguous United States, most especially in California and the northwestern states
Food: The caterpillar eats plants from the rose family (Rosaceae), ceanothus, willow, and aspen. Adults do not feed.
Description: The Sheep Moth, also known as the Elegant Sheep Moth, is a silk moth of the West that can be found flying during the day. The wing pattern and coloration is extremely variable. Generally, it is rosy to pink on the forewing and yellow orange on the hindwing, with both wings showing large, central black spots, marginal streaks, and transverse bands. In some regions, however, the dark markings are more extensive, reduced, or entirely absent. The underside wings are patterned as above. The body is long for a silk moth, with a thin abdomen. It is yellow to pinkish with a black-banded abdomen and feathered antennae (broader in the male). The caterpillar is blackish, often with dorsal red spots and white lines along the sides, and has rows of highly branched orange and black spines. The illustration shows the male.

MOTHS

Io Moth, *Automeris io*
Family Saturniidae (Giant Silk Moths)
Size: Wingspan 2–3.25"
Habitat: Deciduous woodlands, parks, gardens
Range: Throughout the contiguous United States, especially in central and eastern states
Food: The caterpillar eats a wide variety of plants, including corn, roses, clover, maple, and birch. Adults do not feed.

Description: The Io Moth is a medium-to-large silk moth named after a mythical Greek maiden, or perhaps a moon of Jupiter, and is also known as the Bull's Eye Moth because of its large, circular eyespots. Males and females exhibit very different coloration. In the female, the forewings are reddish brown to purplish with indistinct, paler scalloping and darker marks; when lifted forward they reveal a hindwing with an alarming, large, black eyespot set against a bright yellow background. Males have yellow forewings marked with brown, with a similar eyespot on the hindwing and a patch of red orange at the base that merges with a red submarginal band. The body is plump and heavily furred, yellow in males, reddish brown in females. The antennae of the male are more heavily feathered. The caterpillar is light green with a red and white stripe along each side, and is covered in greenish-yellow, well-branched, stinging spines. The male is illustrated.

Carolina Sphinx, *Manduca sexta*

Family Sphingidae (Sphinx and Hawk Moths)

Size: Wingspan 4–4.75"

Habitat: Agricultural fields, rural gardens

Range: Most of the contiguous United States except for northwest and north-central states

Food: The caterpillar eats plants from the nightshade family (Solanaceae), including tobacco, potatoes, and tomatoes. The adult feeds on flower nectar with its extremely long tongue (proboscis), allowing it to probe deep into tubular flowers.

Description: As a group, the sphinx moths (also called hawk moths) are known for their long, narrow wings, large bodies, and fast, strong flight. The Carolina Sphinx is very well camouflaged, being almost undetectable when settled on tree bark. Both wings are finely mottled in grays, browns, and white, with small white spots on the margins and congealed dark bands on the hindwing. The body is huge compared to the wings, is brownish on the head and thorax, has six pairs of square, orange spots on each side of the abdomen, and has long, feathered antennae. The caterpillar, called the tobacco hornworm because of the damage it causes to tobacco and other crops, is large, green with oblique white stripes along the sides, and has a prominent orange tail horn.

MOTHS

Pink-spotted Hawkmoth, *Agrius cingulata*

Family Sphingidae (Sphinx and Hawk Moths)
Size: Wingspan 3.5–4.75"
Habitat: Open fields, gardens
Range: Throughout the contiguous United States, most commonly in lower latitudes
Food: The caterpillar eats sweet potato and jimsonweed. The adult feeds on flower nectar with an extremely long tongue (proboscis), which allows it to probe deep into tubular flowers. Adults can also feed while hovering.
Description: The Pink-spotted Hawkmoth, similar in shape and habits to the Carolina Sphinx, has long, narrow wings, a relatively thick, long body, and powerful flight. The forewing is cryptically patterned in an intricate design of gray, brown, black and white, which forms a perfect camouflage on tree bark when the wings are lowered. The hindwing is grayish with black bands and flushed with pink at the base. The robust body, which has a pointed tail end, is a mottled gray brown with distinct pink spots along the sides of the abdomen. The antennae are long, pale, and feathered. The caterpillar, known as the sweet potato hornworm, can be a pest to crops. It is large, smooth, green to brown or nearly black with pale, oblique stripes along the sides, and has a tail horn.

MOTHS

Twin-spotted Sphinx, *Smerinthus jamaicensis*
Family Sphingidae (Sphinx and Hawk Moths)
Size: Wingspan 2–3"
Habitat: A variety of habitats including woodlands, riparian areas, gardens
Range: Throughout the contiguous United States, less commonly in the far West
Food: The caterpillar eats a variety of plants, including wild cherry, apple, birch, elm, and willow. Adults do not feed.
Description: The Twin-spotted Sphinx is a medium-size hawk moth with the large body and long, narrow wings typical of this family. The forewings have an undulating outer margin with a shallow notch at the tip. In males, the upperside of the forewing is mottled pale gray overall with black markings near the center and a dark crescent at the apex. Females are patterned similarly but are colored tan to brownish. The hindwing of both sexes is rosy red at the base with broad, pale-gray or yellowish margins and has a large, blue-centered, black eyespot that may be divided into two blue spots. The body is robust, brownish gray, with a black patch over the head and thorax, and feathered antennae, which are larger and bushier in the male. Males tend to rest with the abdomen arched upward. The caterpillar is fat, green with tiny white dots, shows oblique, pale yellow stripes along the sides, and has a short tail horn. The male is illustrated.

White-lined Sphinx, *Hyles lineata*

Family Sphingidae (Sphinx and Hawk Moths)

Size: Wingspan 2.5–3.5"

Habitat: A variety of habitats including fields, gardens, dry scrub

Range: Widespread throughout the contiguous United States

Food: The caterpillar eats a variety of plants, including apple, elm, evening primrose, and tomato. Adults feed on flower nectar, using their very long proboscises to probe deep into flowers.

Description: The White-lined Sphinx, worldwide in distribution, is sometimes referred to as the Striped Morning Sphinx because it flies during the day as well as night. It is large bodied with a tapered abdomen and pointed, narrow wings. The upperside of the forewing is tan and dark brown with a broad pale stripe from the wing base to the tip, crossed by broad, white veins. The hindwing is mostly pink with black at the base and just inside the outer margin. The underside wings are paler overall. The upper thorax and head of the body are brownish with white stripes while the abdomen has black-and-white spotting along the top and sides. The antennae are long with compact feathering. The caterpillar is plump, smooth, and blackish; shows variable amounts of yellow or green stripes and spots; and has a prominent, yellow-orange tail horn.

Hummingbird Clearwing, *Hemaris thysbe*

Family Sphingidae (Sphinx and Hawk Moths)
Size: Wingspan 1.5–2.5″
Habitat: Gardens, meadows, roadsides
Range: From Alaska to Florida, most commonly in the eastern United States, and rarely in the Southwest
Food: The caterpillar eats a variety of plants, including hawthorn, honeysuckle, cherry, plum, and snowberry. The adults feeds on flower nectar, using a long proboscis to probe deep into flowers.
Description: The Hummingbird Clearwing is a common, medium-size hawk moth that is active during the day and resembles a small hummingbird with its rapid, hovering flight and compact body shape. The forewings are narrow and pointed, are reddish brown with olive green at the base, and have large, clear, scaleless patches along their central sections. The hindwings are much smaller and rounded, with similar clear patches. The body is robust, olive green above on the thorax and head, whitish below, with a dark reddish brown to blackish abdomen that terminates in a broad tail tuft. The antennae are long, thick, and black. The caterpillar is fat and bright green, with longitudinal pale stripes and a single, yellow to bluish tail horn.

Double-toothed Prominent, *Nerice bidentata*

Family Notodontidae (Prominents)
Size: Wingspan 1.25–1.5"
Habitat: Deciduous woodlands, parks, habitats where elm is found
Range: Throughout eastern United States
Food: The caterpillar eats the leaves of elms and related species.

Description: The Double-toothed Prominent is a small, common moth of the east with broad wings and scales at the basal edge of the forewings; these stand upright, hence the name "prominent." The upperside of the forewing is brown along the top half, grayish on the bottom half, with a ragged, dark, double-toothed edge in between. The hindwing is an unmarked brown, paler toward the base. With wings folded flat or angled as a tent, the moth appears convincingly as a strip of bark or dry leaves. The body is mottled pale gray brown and has heavily furred legs and feathered antennae. The caterpillar, known as the elm caterpillar, is small and green, with pale stripes above, yellow lines along the sides, and several raised, forked ridges along the back.

Eight-spotted Forester, *Alypia octomaculata*
Family Noctuidae (Forester, Dagger, and Cutworm Moths)
Size: Wingspan 1–1.5"
Habitat: Open woodlands, fields, riparian areas, urban parks
Range: Throughout the contiguous United States, more commonly in the East
Food: The caterpillar eats a variety of plants, including grape, Virginia creeper, woodvine, and peppervine. Adults feed on flower nectar.
Description: The Eight-spotted Forester is a small, boldly patterned moth with strong flight that is active during the day. The upperside wings are rich black overall, with two large, pale-yellow spots on the forewing and two large, white spots on the hindwing, although there may be variation in the number and size of these markings. The undersides of the wings are patterned as above. The body is black overall, with pale yellow sides to the thorax, variably occuring white spotting on top of the abdomen, bright orange tufts on the front two legs, and dark antennae that are thickened toward the tip but not noticeably feathered. The caterpillar is black with broad orange bands and thin, broken, white bands, and is spiked with thin, pale hairs.

MOTHS

Dingy Cutworm Moth, *Feltia jaculifera*

Family Noctuidae (Forester, Dagger, and Cutworm Moths)
Size: Wingspan 1.25–1.5"
Habitat: Most open areas, gardens, native grasslands, farms, meadows
Range: Throughout most of the contiguous United States except for the southwestern region
Food: The caterpillar eats a wide variety of herbaceous plants, including grasses, alfalfa, corn, and goldenrod. Adults feed on the nectar of flowers, especially those in the sunflower family (Compositae).
Description: The Dingy Cutworm Moth, a small, common nocturnal moth, is also known as the Bent-line Dart because it exhibits erratic, darting flight when alarmed. The upperside of the forewing has a complex pattern of browns, grays, blacks, and whites, and, most distinctively, two whitish bands that originate at the base and diverge past several interior, angular, black marks. The hindwing is dull gray brown with a lighter margin. At rest, the wings are typically held close together and angled like a roof. The body is pale grayish brown with darker marks on the upper thorax and long, thin, feathered antennae. The caterpillar gives this moth its more common name, as it is a rather dingy, mottled gray or pale brown, with dark lines on either side of the back. It can be a major pest to crops because it feeds by cutting plant stems near their bases.

American Dagger Moth, *Acronicta americana*
Family Noctuidae (Forester, Dagger, and Cutworm Moths)
Size: Wingspan 2–2.5"
Habitat: Deciduous woodlands, swamps
Range: Throughout eastern United States
Food: The caterpillar eats a wide variety of deciduous trees, including elm, willow, oak, walnut, alder, and maple.
Description: The American Dagger Moth, a medium-size moth with pale, cryptic coloration, is a member of the group known as dagger moths, so called because of the pointed, thin, dark marks on their forewings that resemble little daggers. The upperside of the forewing is mottled in shades of gray or gray brown with various darker marks, and has a jagged postmedial line with a black "dagger" mark near the bottom margin. The hindwings are brownish with pale margins. The wing undersides are more uniform in color, with a distinct dark spot in the center of the hindwing. The body is a mottled pale gray brown that matches the color of the wings and enhances the moth's excellent camouflage as tree bark. The antennae are relatively thin and short. The caterpillar is densely covered with long, whitish to pale-yellow bristles, and has two pairs of very long, tufted black hairs on the front end and a single black bristle near the hind end. The head is black. Caution is advised when handling, as the bristles may irritate the skin.

MOTHS

Giant Leopard Moth, *Hypercompe scribonia*
Family Erebidae (Tiger Moths and Allies)
Size: Wingspan 2.5–3.5"
Habitat: Woodland edges
Range: Eastern United States, west to Texas and north to the Great Lakes region
Food: The caterpillar eats a wide variety of herbaceous and woody plants, including cherry, mustard, plantain, lilac, dandelion, and willow.
Description: The Giant Leopard Moth is a striking, medium-to-large moth (one of the largest of the tiger moths) that flies at night and is readily attracted to lights. The upperside of the fore-wing is white and uniformly covered with solid or open black spots. The hindwing is mostly unmarked white but has a deep yellow-and-brown basal margin and variable dark spots at the outer margin. The underside is patterned as above. The head and thorax repeat the black spotting on the forewings and are white below. When the wings are spread, the conspicuous bluish-black, orange-spotted abdomen is revealed. The antennae are bluish black and very thin. The caterpillar is fat and covered in long, black bristles, which usually hide the red bands at each segment. In defense, it will curl into a ball, upon which the red bands are visible.

Garden Tiger Moth, *Arctia caja*

Family Erebidae (Tiger Moths and Allies)

Size: Wingspan 2–2.75"

Habitat: A variety of habitats, especially damp areas, meadows, and streamsides

Range: Primarily the Pacific Northwest and Rocky Mountains, but also found in north-central and northeastern states

Food: The caterpillar eats a wide variety of herbaceous and woody plants, including blackberry, clover, plum, plantain, birch, and apple.

Description: The Garden Tiger Moth is a beautiful, medium-size tiger moth with nocturnal habits and quite variable wing coloration. In general, the upperside of the forewing consists of a contrasting mosaic of reddish or dark-brown patches over a white background. The hindwing is bright orange with large, black-rimmed blue spots and a pale margin. With the forewings folded down, the butterfly is camouflaged in grasses and brush, but when alarmed it flashes its brilliant hindwings to frighten predators. The body is dark brown above on the head and thorax, with a red collar at the neck, and is orange with broken, dark blue bands on the abdomen. It is mostly brownish-orange below with pale, compact antennae. The caterpillar is of the "woolly bear" type, densely covered in long, pale-tipped black bristles with shorter reddish bristles near the base and at the neck.

MOTHS

Gypsy Moth, *Lymantria dispar*
Family Erebidae (Tiger Moths and Allies)
Size: Wingspan 1.25–2.5"
Habitat: Deciduous woodlands
Range: Northeastern United States
Food: The Gypsy Moth caterpillar is considered a serious pest as it feeds voraciously on a wide variety of trees and shrubs, including oak, apple, willow, birch, larch, and roses. Adults do not feed.
Description: The Gypsy Moth is an introduced species from Europe, and is now common across the northeast and steadily increasing its range. It is a small- to medium-size moth, with females being larger than males, unable to fly, and different in coloration. The forewing of males is mottled with shades of brown and black, with a darker outer margin and small black marks near the leading edge. The hindwing is unmarked reddish brown. Females are white overall with thin, gray, zigzag lines across the wings, small black marks near the leading edge of the forewing, and dark, square spots at the outer margin of both wings. The body is brownish with a thin abdomen in males, white with a thick abdomen in females, and has a bushy upper thorax region in both sexes. The antennae in males have very wide feathering, while those of the female are rather thin. The caterpillar is grayish, covered in long hairs, and has both blue and red spots along the back.

Isabella Tiger Moth, *Pyrrhartia isabella*

Family Erebidae (Tiger Moths and Allies)

Size: Wingspan 1.75–2.5"

Habitat: Open, deciduous woodlands, grasslands, gardens, parks

Range: Throughout the contiguous United States

Food: The caterpillar eats a wide variety of herbaceous and woody plants, including maples, clover, sunflowers, elm, and grasses.

Description: The Isabella Tiger Moth is a common, medium-size moth, most often known by its larval form, the woolly bear caterpillar. The adult has relatively long, pointed forewings, which are colored light yellow brown overall and sparsely marked with faint bars near the outer and medial sections. There are also variable numbers of small, dark spots on the interior and outer margin. The hindwing of the female is tinged orange to pink, whereas that of the male is pale yellow. The body is orange brown with a hairy, tufted, upper thorax; dark spots along the upper abdomen; thin, pale antennae; and black legs. The caterpillar is plump and covered with fuzzy, fine hairs. It is black with a wide, orange-brown central section.

MOTHS

Clymene, *Haploa clymene*
Family Erebidae (Tiger Moths and Allies)
Size: Wingspan 1.5–2"
Habitat: Deciduous woodlands, moist fields
Range: Eastern states, west to Texas and north to the Great Lakes
Food: The caterpillar eats the leaves of willow, oak, and plants in the sunflower family (Compositae).
Description: Named after the mythical Greek goddess of fame, the Clymene is an elegantly patterned, medium-size tiger moth that is active both day and night. The upperside of the forewing is bright to creamy white with broad black marks near the leading edge, and both outer and inner margins. With wings folded, the central black mark resembles a dagger. The hindwing is bright orange, yellow, or white, with a large dark spot near the lower margin (sometimes this is accompanied by an additional, smaller spot). The underside is a relatively unpatterned rusty brown. The body is cream on the thorax and yellow orange on the head and abdomen, with a dark dorsal stripe running the length of the body; it is uniformly reddish brown below. The antennae are long, black, and thin, and the legs are black. The caterpillar is mostly black with sparse, fine, pale hairs and rows of yellow spots along the sides.

Dogbane Tiger Moth, *Cycnia tenera*
Family Erebidae (Tiger Moths and Allies)
Size: Wingspan 1.25–1.75"
Habitat: Meadows, roadsides, fields where dogbane is present
Range: Throughout the contiguous United States, most commonly in eastern states
Food: The caterpillar eats the leaves of the dogbane plant, milkweed, and Indian hemp.
Description: Also known as the Delicate Cycnia, the Dogbane Tiger Moth is a small- to medium-size, ghostly, mostly nocturnal moth. It has the ability to communicate with other moths by echolocation, which is also thought to confuse bats who might prey on them. The uppersides of the wings are pure white and nearly translucent, including the veins, except for a butter-yellow to golden strip along the leading edge of the forewing. The undersides are colored the same, with the addition of a dusky flush to the forewing just under the yellow strip. The head and sides of the thorax are bright yellow, the rest of the body is white, and there is a strip of black spots and yellow bands along the top and sides of the abdomen. The antennae are thin and lined black and white, as are the legs. The caterpillar is white to very pale brown or gray and covered in long, soft hairs that arise from branching, basal tufts.

MOTHS

White Underwing, *Catocala relicta*
Family Erebidae (Tiger Moths and Allies)
Size: Wingspan 2.75–3.25"
Habitat: Deciduous woodlands
Range: Midwestern and northeastern United States
Food: The caterpillar eats the leaves of willow, aspen, and poplar.

Description: The White Underwing is a medium- to large-size, nocturnal, cryptically patterned moth. Its name reflects the sudden appearance of its boldly colored, white-striped hindwing when the forewing is raised—a move thought to startle predators. Another common name for this species is the Relict. The forewing has a white or pale-gray background color overlaid with variable amounts of dark gray, gray brown, or black marks and parallel scalloped lines. The hindwing is black with a distinct white medial band and a white marginal band. The body is furry and robust, white below and black or dark brown above, with black-and-white-banded legs, and very thin, long antennae. The caterpillar is pale gray with a black head, small black spots at the side of each segment, and a dark smudge near the midsection. It is smooth except for a row of hairs lining the base.

Bella Moth, *Utetheisa ornatrix*

Family Erebidae (Tiger Moths and Allies)
Size: Wingspan 1.25–1.75"
Habitat: Fields, meadows, woodland edges
Range: Across eastern and southern United States, most commonly in the south
Food: The caterpillar eats a variety of plants in the pea family (Fabaceae), especially rattlebox (Crotalaria).
Description: Also known as the Ornate Moth or the Rattlebox Moth, the Bella Moth is a beautiful little tiger moth that is active during the day and exhibits a considerable amount of variation in color, depending on its range. In the more common form (bella form), the upperside of the forewing is orange to yellowish brown, with transverse rows of white-bordered, black spots, while the hindwing is bright pink with an irregular black marginal band. In a less common form found in the southern part of its range, the forewing is much paler to nearly white with a few black spots, and the hindwing is mostly white with the same black marginal patch. The wings are often pulled tightly together behind the back, giving them a tentlike appearance. The body is mostly white with black spots on the thorax and sides of the abdomen, and the head has thin, dark antennae. The caterpillar is stout, colored with alternating bands of black and orange, and has very sparse, long hairs and has a glossy, red head. The bella form is illustrated.

MOTHS

The Neighbor, *Haploa contigua*
Family Erebidae (Tiger Moths and Allies)
Size: Wingspan 1.5–2"
Habitat: Open, deciduous woodlands, riparian areas, marshes
Range: Midwestern and east-central states
Food: The caterpillar eats the leaves of a variety of trees, including poplar, wild plum, willow, hazelnut, and apple.
Description: The Neighbor is a medium-size tiger moth with somewhat long, narrow wings. The upperside of the forewings is creamy white with a bold, geometric overlay of broad, black marks at each margin and in the outer, central section. This patterning effectively breaks up the outline of the moth, and is scientifically known as a "disruptive" pattern that may confuse predators. The hindwings are uniformly white. The body is white with a reddish orange head, a black dorsal stripe on the thorax and abdomen, and thin, stringy antennae. The caterpillar is dark gray above, pale yellow along the sides, and dotted with black bumps that give rise to thin, branching spines.

MOTHS

Black Witch, *Ascalapha odorata*
Family Erebidae (Tiger Moths and Allies)
Size: Wingspan 4–6″
Habitat: Open fields, urban areas
Range: Throughout the United States, including Hawaii, excepting Alaska, and most commonly in Florida and southern Texas
Food: The caterpillar eats the leaves of a variety of plants from the pea family (Fabaceae), including acacia, cassia, mesquite, and locust. The adult feeds on flower nectar and rotting fruit.

Description: The Black Witch is a very large, nocturnal moth whose long, pointed forewings, strong flight, and dark shape give the impression of a small bat. There is much folklore concerning doom and foreboding to those who are visited by this moth. The wings are overall rich brown, intricately scalloped, and mottled with shades of tan and violet. The forewing bears a distinct, kidney-shaped, iridescent blue spot ringed with black and red, which is found near the center of the discal cell. The hindwing is squared off, wavy at its lower margin, and bears large, double eyespots. In females there is a pale, pinkish band running across the center of both wings. The body is heavily furred, colored various shades of brown, and has long, thin antennae. The caterpillar is dark brown and smooth, with three pale blotches across the back.

MOTHS

Virginia Ctenucha, *Ctenucha virginica*
Family Erebidae (Tiger Moths and Allies)
Size: Wingspan 1.5–2"
Habitat: Marshes, meadows, fields with flowers
Range: Midwestern and northeastern United States
Food: The caterpillar eats a variety of plants including grasses, sedges, and irises.
Description: The Virginia Ctenucha is a member the group known as wasp moths because of their physical resemblance to wasps and diurnal behavior. The forewings are narrow, rounded at the tips, uniformly brownish to charcoal gray, and fringed with white. Some blue from the thorax may encroach upon the basal area. The hindwings are uniformly black, fringed white, but are rarely visible since they stay tucked in below the forewings. The undersides are pale brown. The head and neck area is bright orange, the thorax and abdomen are iridescent blue above and below, and the antennae are dark, very long, and broadly feathered.

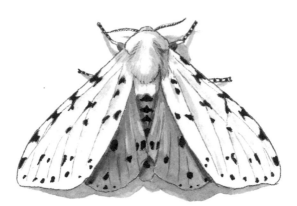

Salt Marsh Moth, *Estigmene acrea*
Family Erebidae (Tiger Moths and Allies)
Size: Wingspan 1.75–2.75"
Habitat: Meadows, fields, fresh and saltwater marshes, open woodlands
Range: Throughout the contiguous United States, most commonly in central and eastern states
Food: The caterpillar eats a variety of herbaceous plants, including clover, pea, cotton, mallow, cabbage, and pigweed, as well as trees such as walnut and apple.
Description: Also known as the Acrea Moth, the Salt Marsh Moth is a nocturnal moth that may be found in many areas other than salt marshes. The upperside of the forewing is white with numerous, small, scattered black marks, sometimes showing a black strip along the leading edge. The hindwing in the female is white, while in the male it is yellow to orange, with both sexes showing three or more black marks. This moth often holds its wings in a tight, angled, tentlike posture. The body is robust, with a broad, well-furred, white thorax and head, and an orange abdomen with black spots along the back (tipped with white in the female). The legs are banded in black and white, as are the narrow, feathered antennae. The caterpillar, known as the salt marsh caterpillar, is covered in tufts of fine hairs, ranging from light to dark brown, with orange or black warts along the back. The male is illustrated.

MOTHS

White-marked Tussock Moth, *Orygia leucostigma*

Family Erebidae (Tiger Moths and Allies)
Size: Wingspan 1–1.5″ (male)
Habitat: Deciduous and coniferous woodlands, rural gardens
Range: Throughout eastern United States
Food: The caterpillar eats the leaves of a variety of plants from the pea family (Fabaceae), including acacia, cassia, mesquite, and locust. The adult feeds on flower nectar and rotting fruit.

Description: The White-marked Tussock Moth is a small, nocturnal, cryptically colored moth, and the female of the species is wingless. In the male, the upperside of the forewing is mottled in shades of brown and gray, with some dark, scalloped lines along the mid-section that enclose a broad, pale band, variable black markings and patches, and a white spot near the lower edge. The hindwing is uniformly gray brown. The body of the male is mottled gray and brown, with long hairs on the legs and very long feathering on the antennae. The body of the female is whitish to pale gray with small antennae. The caterpillar is quite bizarre in appearance. The body is striped yellow and black with long, fine hairs and a bright red, round head. Clumps of hairs shaped like a bottle brush (the "tussocks") cover the forward part of the back, there is a long, hairy tail projection, and two long, black tufts arise from the head. Contact with the hairs can cause irritation to the skin.

Skiff Moth, *Prolimacodes badia*

Family Limacodidae (Slug Caterpillar Moths)
Size: Wingspan 1–1.25"
Habitat: Deciduous woodlands
Range: Throughout eastern United States
Food: The caterpillar eats a variety of shrubs and trees, including cherry, birch, willow, oak, and poplar.
Description: The Skiff Moth is a small, nocturnal moth with a clean, bold wing pattern. The upperside of the forewing is simply patterned with a background of pale brown, which forms a contrasting background to a dark, chestnut-brown, white-bordered patch that forms a semicircle along the leading edge. The hindwing is uniformly brown, and the wings are often folded tightly across the back in a tentlike fashion. The body is furry and robust, with a wide thorax; brown coloring; long, thin antennae; and white spots on otherwise brown legs. The caterpillar, which shows an overall green color, moves like a slug, with suckers for feet instead of normal legs. It is smooth, hunchbacked, and has a pointed tail and two brown spots on the top. Overall it gives the appearance of a folded-over green leaf.

MOTHS

Yellow-shouldered Slug Moth, *Lithacodes fasciola*

Family Limacodidae (Slug Caterpillar Moths)

Size: Wingspan .75–1"

Habitat: Deciduous woodlands, gardens

Range: Throughout eastern United States

Food: The caterpillar eats the leaves of a variety of deciduous trees, including elm, maple, oak, apple, and willow.

Description: Also known as the Ochre-winged Hag Moth, the Yellow-shouldered Slug Moth is a tiny moth in the group of slug caterpillar moths, with a larvae that is shaped like and moves like a slug. In the adult, the upperside of the forewing is deep ochre to orange brown with a jagged white medial stripe, bordered distally by a wide gray band that bleeds into a thin, oblique dark line near the outer margin. The hindwing is a uniformly pale ochre washed with gray. The body is furry and yellowish to reddish brown overall, with thin, pale, long antennae. This moth is distinctive in its curious habit of arching its back so the tip of the abdomen points nearly straight up. The caterpillar, like others in this family, has a flattened bottom surface with disclike feet, allowing it to creep like a slug. It is oval, shiny, brilliant yellow green, about half an inch long when mature, and is covered in small bumps and craters.

Large Maple Spanworm Moth, *Prochoerodes lineola or P. transversata*

Family Geometridae (Looper or Geometer Moths)
Size: Wingspan 1.25–2"
Habitat: Deciduous and mixed woodlands, grassy fields
Range: Throughout eastern United States
Food: The caterpillar eats a wide variety of woody and herbaceous plants, including maple, apple, oak, cherry, walnut, and grasses.
Description: The Large Maple Spanworm Moth is a medium-size, nocturnal moth in the group of geometer or looper moths, so called because the caterpillar moves by bringing its back legs toward the head, forming a loop, then stretching the front legs forward. The uppersides of both wings show variable shades of earthy colors, including brown, ochre, orange, cream, and brownish green—all colors seen in dried, late-summer leaves, which the moth resembles. Cutting across both wings, from wingtip to wingtip, is a thin, dark, transverse line. There also may be dark, zigzag markings on either side of this line. The body is brownish above, matching the wing color, and paler below, with a relatively slender abdomen and thin, feathered antennae. The caterpillar resembles a stiff, leafless twig. Called a spanworm, or inchworm, it is thin and mottled in browns and grays.

MOTHS

Pale Beauty, *Campaea perlata*

Family Geometridae (Looper or Geometer Moths)

Size: Wingspan 1–2"

Habitat: Deciduous and coniferous woodlands, shrubby fields

Range: Across the northern half of the United States, including Alaska, and Canada from British Columbia to Nova Scotia

Food: The caterpillar eats a wide variety of trees and shrubs, including conifers, alder, aspen, elm, willow, and blueberry.

Description: The Pale Beauty is a small- to medium-size nocturnal moth able to survive in arctic climates. It rests with its wings spread and flat, revealing nearly the entire hindwing. The wings are thin, translucent, and range from white to grayish to pale green. Like the Large Maple Spanworm, it has a dark line that traverses wingtip to wingtip across the center of both wings, with the addition of a second line closer to the base on the forewing. The body is uniformly pale, matching the color of the wings, interrupted only by the black eyes. It has a slender abdomen, and the legs and the thin antennae are white. The caterpillar, sometimes called the "fringed looper," is mottled in grays and brown, and lined with pale fringes along the base on either side of the body. Like other members of the looper moth family, the caterpillar uses an inchworm style of locomotion. It is very well camouflaged, looking like a lichen on a rock.

Eastern Tent Caterpillar Moth, *Malacosoma americanum*
Family Lasiocampidae (Tent Caterpillar Moths)
Size: Wingspan 1–1.75"
Habitat: Deciduous woodlands, orchards, gardens
Range: Across eastern United States
Food: The caterpillar eats the leaves of plants and trees in the rose family (Rosaceae), including apple, cherry, crabapple, and plum. Adults do not feed.

Description: The Eastern Tent Caterpillar Moth is a common, nocturnal, small- to medium-size moth with a wide body and stubby wings. The forewings are pale gray brown to rich, reddish, or chocolate brown, with two white stripes across the interior that sometimes enclose a paler band. The outer wing margins are white and checkered with brown spots; the hindwing is uniformly brown. The body is robust and furry, especially on the thorax, and shows light-to-dark-brown coloration with a slight dark band on the abdomen. The antennae are brown, broad, and feathered. The caterpillar gets its name by spinning silken threads from which it constructs a protective tentlike structure in the forks of branches. It is grayish, marked with blue and red, has a white dorsal stripe, and is covered in fine, long hairs. Periodic infestations of this caterpillar can cause much harm to orchard crops.

Evergreen Bagworm Moth, *Thyridopteryx ephemeraeformis*
Family Psychidae (Bagworm Moths)
Size: Wingspan .75–1.3"
Habitat: Deciduous, mixed, or coniferous woodlands, parks, gardens
Range: Across the United States east of the Continental Divide
Food: The caterpillar eats primarily conifers, including spruce, pine, juniper, and cedar, but will also eat hardwoods such as locust and sycamore. It is considered a pest on ornamental evergreen trees.

Description: The Evergreen Bagworm Moth is a small moth with an unusual lifestyle and extreme sexual dimorphism. The male resembles a large, long-bodied fly or a dark-colored wasp, with its black, furry body; stubby, clear wings; and thick, feathered antennae. The female resembles a whitish, furry worm. Lacking wings, legs, eyes and antennae, she remains in a silken bag with the sole purpose of accepting a mate and breeding. The caterpillar is smooth and mottled in brown, black, and white. It combines silken threads with bits of foliage to form a sac which it drags along until pupation. The sac is then fixed to a branch and hangs like a small cone.

Carpenterworm Moth, *Prionoxystus robiniae*
Family Cossidae (Carpenter Moths)
Size: Wingspan 1.75–3.25"
Habitat: Deciduous woodlands, rural areas with host tree species
Range: Throughout the contiguous United States
Food: The caterpillar eats a variety of broadleaf trees, including oak, willow, locust, ash, and maple. It bores tunnels into the wood of these trees and feeds therein, and can cause much damage to lumber trees.
Description: The Carpenterworm Moth is a large, nocturnal moth with a relatively large body; long, narrow, triangular forewings; and reduced hindwings that are similar to those of sphinx moths. The forewings are translucent and intricately mottled and spotted in dark gray and white. The hindwing of males is blackish near the base and margin and yellow orange at the outer half. In females, the hindwing is mostly black. The body is mottled dark gray and white, matching the wing color, and shows a darker abdomen that is quite pointed at the tail end in males but less pointed in females whose tail sections are fatter. The feathered antennae are thick in males and thin in females. The caterpillar, sometimes called the "locust borer," may take three to four years to pupate. It is smooth, ranges from pale green to reddish, and has dark spots along the sides.

Grapeleaf Skeletonizer, *Harrisina americana*
Family Zygaenidae (Skeletonizer Moths)
Size: Wingspan .75–1.25"
Habitat: Meadows, fields, gardens
Range: Throughout eastern United States
Food: The caterpillar eats the leaves of various grape species, Virginia creeper, and redbud.
Description: The Grapeleaf Skeletonizer is a diminutive moth, active both day and night, with a wasplike appearance, having elongated, narrow wings that it holds outstretched. Its name is fitting, as ranks of its larvae, working side by side, can quickly defoliate grapevines. The wings, rounded at the tip, are uniformly steely black and translucent and show black veins. The forewing is twice as long as the hindwing. The body is black with a red-orange collar at the neck, a long abdomen that arches up, a tufted tail end, and thick, feathered antennae (very wide in males). The caterpillar is compact, yellow, banded with black lines or spots, and has white basal stripes. Tiny hairs on its surface may cause skin irritation.

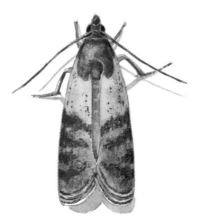

Indian-Meal Moth, *Plodia interpunctella*
Family Pyralidae (Snout Moths)
Size: Wingspan .5–.75"
Habitat: Indoor places with a food source, especially kitchens, pantries, and warehouses, or outside in warm climates. They do not tolerate cold.
Range: Worldwide
Food: The caterpillar eats various grains (especially cornmeal, from which its common name is derived), cereals, dried foods, and pet food. Adults do not feed.
Description: The Indian-Meal Moth is a native of South America that has become naturalized across the globe from the transport of foods that contain its eggs and larvae. It is also known as the Pantry Moth, and is a considerable pest in homes and anywhere dried foods are stored. The adult is tiny, with narrow forewings that are pale gray brown at the base, dark reddish brown on the outer half, and overlaid with broad, broken, charcoal-gray transverse bands. The hindwing is uniformly off-white, but is usually hidden by the tightly folded forewings. The surface of both wings may show a metallic sheen. The body is brown above, gray below, with long, thin antennae. The caterpillar, known as a "waxworm," is smooth and shiny, white, creamy, or pale gray, with a brown head. Feeding caterpillars will leave a residue of silk webbing inside the food source.

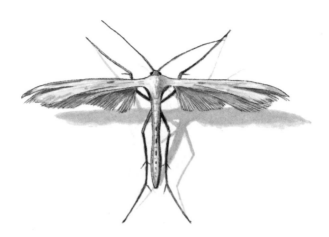

Morning Glory Plume Moth, *Emmelina monodactyla*

Family Pterophoridae (Plume Moths)

Size: Wingspan .75–1"

Habitat: Fields and meadows where host plants are found

Range: Throughout the contiguous United States

Food: The caterpillar eats a variety of herbaceous plants, including bindweeds and morning glorys (Convolvulaceae), lamb's quarters, and members of the nightshade family (Solanaceae).

Description: The Morning Glory Plume Moth is a tiny moth that is active at dusk and has a highly modified body structure. The body is very long and narrow, with long, delicate legs that have thin, pointed spurs. The forewing is deeply cleft into two lobes, each with bristles near the tips. The hindwing is divided into three distinct plumes, each resembling a feather, with fine scales emanating from a central vein. The wings, which are commonly held tightly together and rolled up, appear as a solid stick. The rear legs are often pressed against the body also, giving rise to this moth's other common name, the "T" moth. The color overall is a light to dark brown, interrupted on top of the abdomen with a pale line that may be streaked with darker marks. The caterpillar is pale yellow green with a broad, dark-green stripe down the back, and is covered with fine, pale hairs.

Index

About the Author/Illustrator

Todd Telander is a naturalist/illustrator/artist living in Walla Walla, Washington. He has studied and illustrated wildlife since 1989, while living in California, Colorado, New Mexico, and Washington. He graduated from the University of California at Santa Cruz with degrees in biology, environmental studies, and scientific illustration and has since illustrated numerous books and other publications, including  FalconGuides' Scats and Tracks series. His wife, Kirsten Telander, is a writer, and he has two sons, Miles and Oliver. His work can be viewed online at toddtelander.com.